50 AMAZING DESERT ANIMALS

Real Photos • Incredible Facts for Kids

by Dale Whitman

DYLANNA PUBLISHING

ISBN 978-1-64790-484-5 (paperback)
ISBN 978-1-64790-485-2 (hardcover)

First edition, 2026

For information about bulk discounts, contact:
orders@dylannapublishing.com

Where Are the World's Deserts?

Deserts are found on every continent. Some are hot and sandy, while others are cold and icy—but all deserts receive very little rainfall.

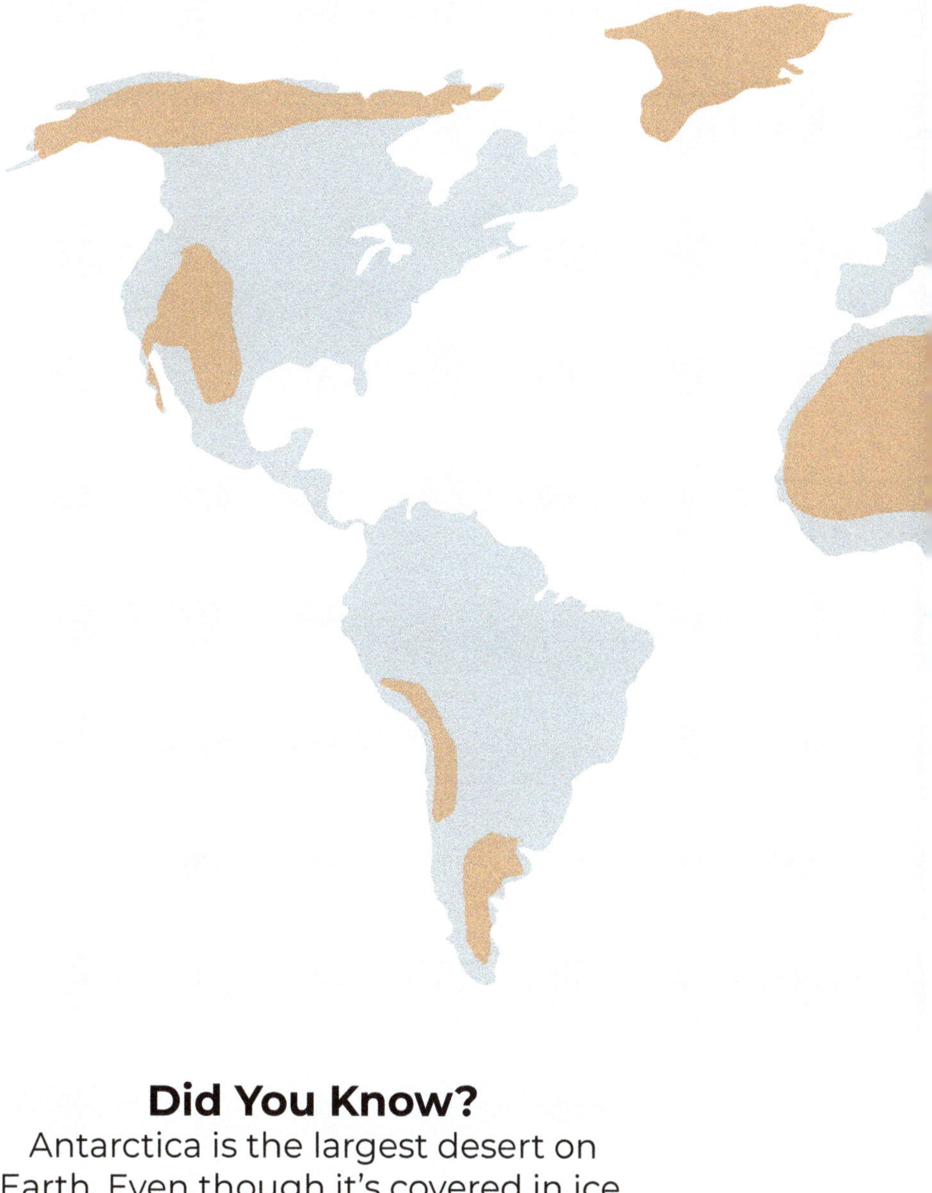

Did You Know?

Antarctica is the largest desert on Earth. Even though it's covered in ice, it receives very little snow each year.

Desert regions are home to animals specially adapted to survive extreme heat, cold, and dryness.

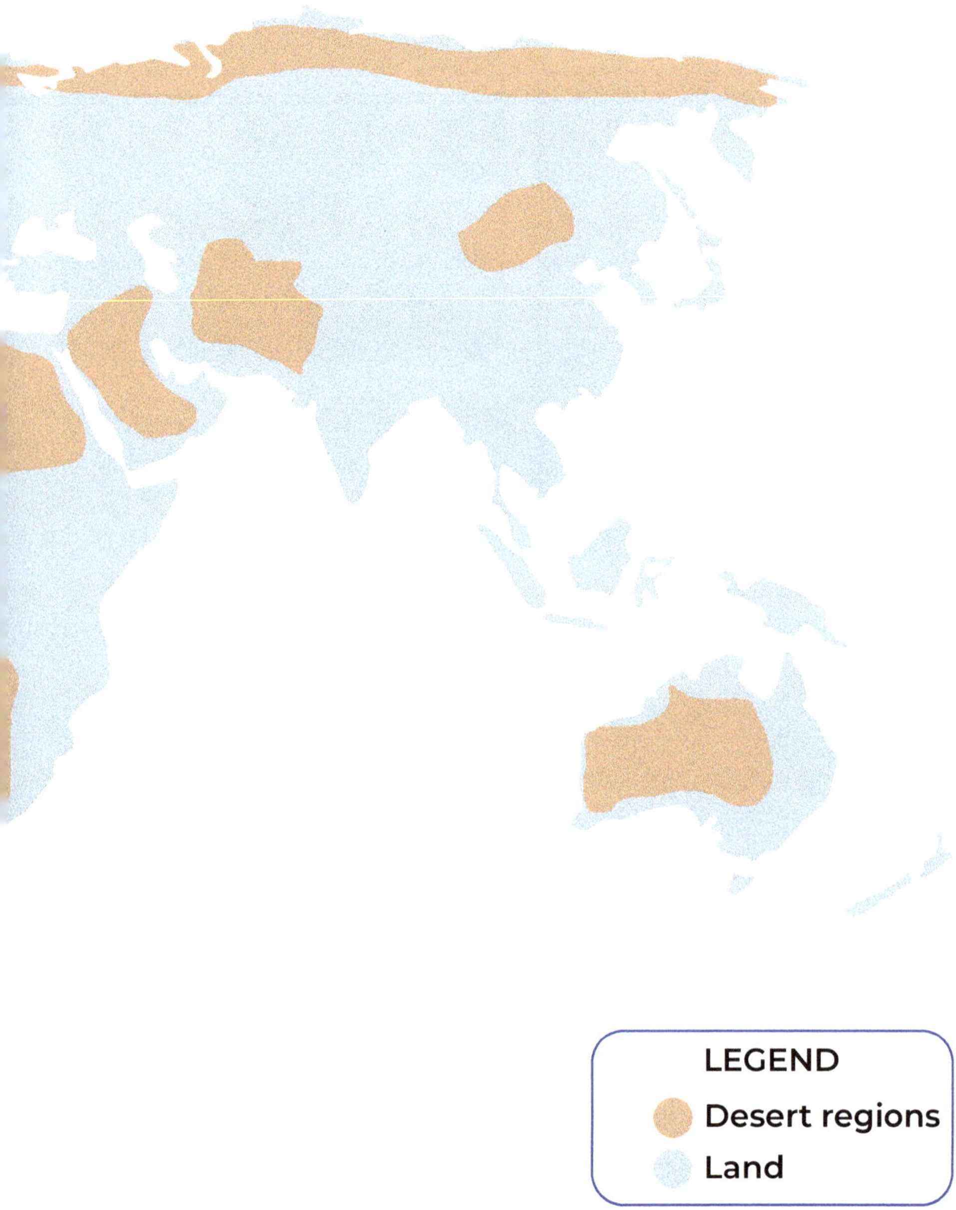

How Desert Animals Survive

Desert animals face two constant challenges: scorching heat and very little water. Over thousands of years, they have developed remarkable solutions to both.

Staying Cool

Many desert animals use large body parts to release heat. The fennec fox's giant ears and the addax's pale coat both work the same way, pushing heat away from the body rather than letting it build up.

Finding Water

Most desert animals never drink at all. The thorny devil collects moisture through its own skin, while the kangaroo rat and jerboa get all the water they need from the seeds they eat.

Blending In

Camouflage helps desert animals hide from predators and ambush prey. The horned lizard disappears against sandy soil, while the sand boa buries itself just below the surface with only its eyes showing.

Storing Energy

When food and water disappear for months, desert animals rely on what they have stored. The camel stores fat in its hump, while the desert tortoise stores water in its bladder.

Moving on Hot Sand

Many desert animals have feet built for hot, loose sand. The sand cat has thick fur on its paws for insulation, while the addax has broad flat hooves that prevent it from sinking into soft ground.

Going Underground

Burrows provide shade, safety, and cooler temperatures. The spadefoot toad can spend nearly a year underground waiting for rain, while the kit fox and kangaroo rat retreat below ground during the hottest part of every day.

Table of Contents

Where Are the World's Deserts? 4

How Desert Animals Survive 6

Welcome to the World of Desert Animals 9

Mammals 10

Reptiles 30

Birds 45

Insects & Arthropods 56

Amphibians 62

Record Breakers 65

Desert Animal Quiz 68

Glossary 70

Index 71

Welcome to the World of Desert Animals

Welcome to the desert, one of the most extreme places on Earth, where life survives against incredible odds.

Imagine a landscape where it barely rains, temperatures swing from scorching hot to freezing cold, and water is more valuable than gold. It may sound impossible for animals to survive, but deserts around the world are home to some of the toughest and most resourceful creatures on the planet.

These animals do more than survive. They thrive. Over time, desert animals have developed incredible adaptations such as storing water in their bodies, hunting at night, and blending into their surroundings. From the tiniest beetle to the tallest camel, each species has its own way of staying alive in a harsh environment.

In this book, you will explore deserts around the world and meet 50 amazing animals that call these places home. The desert may look empty at first glance, but it is full of life for those who know where to look.

WHAT IS A DESERT?

A desert is a place that receives very little precipitation—usually less than 10 inches (25 cm) per year. Deserts can be hot, cold, sandy, rocky, or icy, but they are always dry.

MAMMALS

From tiny mice to giant camels, desert mammals have incredible adaptations for surviving extreme heat and finding water. Their fur, behaviors, and bodies are specially designed to thrive where most animals would perish.

Addax

Addax nasomaculatus

The addax is a rare desert antelope perfectly adapted to life in hot, dry environments. Its broad hooves help it walk on soft sand, and its pale coat keeps it cool. Addax eat tough grasses and shrubs and can go long periods without water. Sadly, they are now critically endangered in the wild.

Habitat:
Sand deserts

Region:
Sahara Desert

Diet:
Herbivore (grasses, shrubs)

Size:
200–300 pounds (90–135 kg)

DID YOU KNOW?
Addax can get all the water they need from plants they eat. Their coat changes color with the seasons to help reflect heat.

2

Arabian Oryx

Oryx leucoryx

The Arabian oryx is a desert antelope known for its long, straight horns and pale coat that reflects sunlight. It can survive extreme heat by lowering its activity during the day. Oryx eat tough desert plants and travel long distances to find food. Once nearly extinct, they are now a major conservation success.

Habitat:
Sand and gravel deserts

Region:
Arabian Peninsula

Diet:
Herbivore (grasses, roots)

Size:
130–160 lbs (59–73 kg)

DID YOU KNOW?

Arabian oryx can detect rain from miles away and travel toward it. They can also survive several days without drinking water.

3

Bactrian Camel

Camelus bactrianus

The Bactrian camel survives in cold deserts with fierce winds and freezing temperatures. Its two humps store fat for long journeys, and its thick winter coat helps it stay warm. These camels eat hardy, salty plants and can handle extremely dry environments. They are some of the toughest mammals on the planet.

Habitat:
Rocky deserts and steppes

Region:
Central Asia

Diet:
Herbivore (grasses, shrubs)

Size:
990–1,100 lbs (450–500 kg)

DID YOU KNOW?
A Bactrian camel can drink up to 30 gallons of water in just 15 minutes after going weeks without any at all. Its two humps can store up to 80 pounds of fat combined.

4

Bighorn Sheep

Ovis canadensis

Bighorn sheep are built for rugged desert mountains, using their specially designed hooves to grip rocky cliffs with ease. Males, called rams, have massive curved horns that can weigh up to 30 pounds, which they use to crash into rivals at full speed during mating season. These sure-footed climbers can escape most predators simply by heading uphill.

Habitat:
Rocky desert slopes

Region:
Southwestern North America

Diet:
Herbivore (shrubs, grasses)

Size:
125–200 lbs (57–91 kg)

DID YOU KNOW?
Bighorn sheep horns are never shed and grow throughout the animal's entire life. Scientists can tell a ram's age by counting the growth rings on its horns, similar to counting tree rings.

Bobcat

Lynx rufus

The bobcat is one of the most elusive hunters in the American desert. Named for its short, stubby tail, this solitary cat ambushes rabbits, rodents, and birds by freezing motionless for long periods before striking. In desert environments, bobcats are rarely seen by humans, preferring to hunt at dawn and dusk when temperatures drop.

Habitat:
Deserts and scrublands

Region:
North America

Diet:
Carnivore (rabbits, rodents, birds)

Size:
15–30 lbs (7–14 kg)

DID YOU KNOW?
A bobcat's spotted coat breaks up its outline so effectively that it can crouch just feet away from prey without being detected.

6

Coyote

Canis latrans

The coyote is one of the most resourceful animals in North America, thriving in open deserts, scrublands, and grasslands across the continent. These clever canines eat nearly anything available: rabbits, rodents, fruit, insects, and carrion. Coyotes communicate through a remarkable mix of howls, yips, and barks, and their calls are one of the most recognizable sounds of the American desert night.

Habitat:
Deserts and grasslands

Region:
North America

Diet:
Omnivore (rabbits, fruit, insects)

Size:
20–50 lbs (9–23 kg)

DID YOU KNOW?
Coyotes now live in every U.S. state excluding Hawaii, making them one of the few wild animals to actually thrive as human cities expanded around them.

Desert Cottontail

Sylvilagus audubonii

The desert cottontail is a small, quick rabbit found throughout the American Southwest. It stays cool by resting in the shade during the hottest part of the day and is most active in the early morning and evening. Its large ears help release body heat, and it gets much of the water it needs directly from the plants it eats.

Habitat:
Desert scrub and grasslands

Region:
Southwestern North America

Diet:
Herbivore (grasses, cacti, bark)

Size:
1–3 lbs (0.5–1.4 kg)

DID YOU KNOW?
To avoid leaving a scent trail for predators, desert cottontails will sometimes eat their own droppings to extract any remaining nutrients, then produce a second, cleaner set of waste.

8

Desert Hedgehog

Paraechinus aethiopicus

The desert hedgehog is a tiny insect-eating mammal covered in sharp spines for protection. It curls tightly into a ball when threatened, leaving only its spines exposed. This hedgehog is most active at night when temperatures drop. It searches for insects and small creatures in dry, rocky areas.

Habitat:
Sandy and rocky deserts, scrublands

Region:
North Africa, Middle East

Diet:
Carnivore (insects, small invertebrates)

Size:
10–18 oz (280–510 g)

DID YOU KNOW?
The desert hedgehog is surprisingly immune to venom and can eat scorpions whole without any ill effects. It will also rub toxic substances on its own spines, possibly to deter predators.

9

Dingo

Canis lupus dingo

The dingo is Australia's wild dog and one of the continent's top predators. Dingoes are highly intelligent and hunt both alone and in small packs, taking prey as large as kangaroos. They rarely bark but communicate through howling. Because they have lived in Australia for thousands of years, dingoes play an important role in keeping desert ecosystems balanced.

Habitat:
Deserts and grasslands

Region:
Australia

Diet:
Carnivore (kangaroos, rabbits, lizards)

Size:
22–33 lbs (10–15 kg)

DID YOU KNOW?
Australia built a 3,500-mile fence specifically to keep dingoes away from sheep farms in the south. It is one of the longest structures ever built by humans.

10

Dromedary Camel

Camelus dromedarius

The dromedary camel is built for hot, dry deserts. Its single hump stores fat that provides energy when food is scarce. Long legs keep its body away from hot sand, and thick lips let it eat tough, thorny plants. It can drink large amounts of water at once and travel great distances with little rest.

Habitat:
Sand and rocky deserts

Region:
Middle East, North Africa

Diet:
Herbivore (leaves, grasses, shrubs)

Size:
880–1,320 lbs (400–600 kg)

DID YOU KNOW?
A dromedary can close its nostrils completely to block out blowing sand, and its eyes have three eyelids — including a thin, transparent one that acts like a built-in pair of goggles during sandstorms.

Fennec Fox

Vulpes zerda

The fennec fox is the smallest fox in the world, but it has the biggest ears! These adorable desert dwellers use their enormous ears to stay cool in the scorching Sahara Desert and to hear prey moving underground. Fennec foxes are nocturnal hunters who sleep in dens during the day and hunt insects, rodents, and lizards at night.

Habitat:
Sand deserts

Region:
Northern Africa

Diet:
Omnivore (insects, rodents, plants)

Size:
2–3 lbs (0.9–1.4 kg)

DID YOU KNOW?
A fennec fox's ears can be up to 6 inches long, more than half the length of its entire body! These giant ears help release heat and can hear a beetle walking on sand from several feet away.

12

Javelina

Pecari tajacu

Also called the collared peccary, the javelina looks like a pig but belongs to a completely different animal family. These stocky desert mammals travel in herds and use their tough snouts to dig up roots, cacti, and bulbs, including plants with spines that most animals avoid entirely. Javelinas have scent glands on their backs and rely heavily on smell to communicate and recognize herd members.

Habitat:
Desert scrub and thornscrub

Region:
Southwestern North America

Diet:
Omnivore (cacti, roots, fruit)

Size:
35–60 lbs (16–27 kg)

DID YOU KNOW?

Javelinas have very poor eyesight and rely almost entirely on smell to navigate and communicate. A herd that gets startled can scatter in all directions and then regroup purely by following each other's scent.

13

Jerboa

Jaculus jaculus

The jerboa is one of the most unusual-looking animals in the desert, with a tiny body, extremely long back legs, and a tail longer than its whole body. It moves by leaping like a miniature kangaroo, covering ground quickly to escape predators. Jerboas are nocturnal and rarely drink water, getting all the moisture they need from the seeds and plants they eat.

Habitat:
Sandy and rocky deserts

Region:
North Africa and Central Asia

Diet:
Herbivore (seeds, plants)

Size:
1–3 oz (28–85 g)

DID YOU KNOW?
The jerboa can leap nearly 10 feet in a single bound and its tail tip may act as a decoy, drawing a predator's strike away from its body.

14

Kangaroo Rat

Dipodomys deserti

The kangaroo rat is a master of desert survival. Like the jerboa, it hops on powerful back legs and rarely needs to drink water, producing moisture internally from the dry seeds it eats. Its large cheek pouches carry food back to underground burrows where it stays cool during the day. Kangaroo rats can even escape a striking rattlesnake by kicking sand and leaping away in an instant.

Habitat:
Desert scrub and sandy soil

Region:
Western North America

Diet:
Herbivore (seeds, grasses)

Size:
1–4 oz (28–113 g)

DID YOU KNOW?
A kangaroo rat can escape a striking rattlesnake by kicking sand in its face and leaping away — all in less than a second!

Kit Fox

Vulpes macrotis

The kit fox is the smallest wild canid in North America and a true desert specialist. Its over-sized ears help radiate heat to keep it cool and pick up the faint sounds of prey moving in the dark. Kit foxes are nocturnal hunters that feed on kangaroo rats, rabbits, and insects, and their sandy-colored fur provides excellent camouflage against the desert floor.

Habitat:
Desert and semi-arid scrubland

Region:
Western North America

Diet:
Carnivore (rodents, rabbits, insects)

Size:
3–6 lbs (1.4–2.7 kg)

DID YOU KNOW?
The kit fox has thick fur on the bottom of its paws that insulates its feet from scorching desert sand and leaves almost no tracks behind.

16

Meerkat

Suricata suricatta

Meerkats live in busy social groups that work together to stay safe. They dig long tunnel systems that provide shelter from heat and predators. While some members forage for food, others stand guard and warn the group of danger. Meerkats eat insects, lizards, and roots found in dry, open areas.

Habitat:
Dry savannas and deserts

Region:
Southern Africa

Diet:
Omnivore (insects, scorpions, lizards)

Size:
1–2 lbs (0.5–0.9 kg)

DID YOU KNOW?
Meerkats are immune to scorpion venom and teach their pups to handle live prey safely, starting with already-dead prey and working up gradually.

17

Pallid Bat

Antrozous pallidus

The pallid bat is a desert bat that hunts insects and small animals on the ground instead of catching them in flight. It uses excellent hearing to locate prey like scorpions and beetles at night. During the day, pallid bats rest in caves, rock crevices, or abandoned buildings to escape the heat.

Habitat:
Deserts and rocky areas

Region:
Western North America

Diet:
Carnivore (insects, scorpions)

Size:
0.7–1.3 oz (20–37 g)

DID YOU KNOW?
Unlike most bats, the pallid bat hunts by listening for prey crawling on the ground rather than chasing flying insects through the air.

18

Pronghorn

Antilocapra americana

The pronghorn is one of North America's most distinctive desert mammals, with bold markings, branched horns, and enormous eyes that can spot movement from miles away. Unlike true antelopes, pronghorns shed and regrow their horn sheaths every year. They travel in loose herds across open desert plains and scrublands, feeding on grasses, shrubs, and cacti.

Habitat:
Deserts and open grasslands

Region:
Western North America

Diet:
Herbivore (shrubs, grasses, cacti)

Size:
90–150 lbs (41–68 kg)

DID YOU KNOW?
The pronghorn is the fastest animal in the Western Hemisphere, capable of sustaining speeds of 55 miles per hour for several miles at a stretch.

Sand Cat

Felis margarita

The sand cat is a small, secretive wild cat that lives in dry deserts. Its pale coat blends with sand, and fur-covered paws protect it from hot ground. It spends the day in cool burrows and hunts rodents, lizards, and insects at night. Sand cats can survive long periods without drinking water.

Habitat:
Sandy and rocky deserts

Region:
North Africa and Middle East

Diet:
Carnivore (rodents, birds, reptiles)

Size:
4–8 lbs (1.8–3.6 kg)

DID YOU KNOW?
Sand cats leave almost no tracks because of thick fur on their paws. This makes them extremely difficult to follow in the wild.

REPTILES

From slow-moving tortoises to lightning-fast lizards, desert reptiles are among the most successful survivors on Earth. Their scaly skin locks in moisture, and their cold-blooded bodies run on far less food and water than mammals of the same size.

20

Bearded Dragon

Pogona vitticeps

The bearded dragon is a calm, sturdy lizard that thrives in hot, open deserts. It has a "beard" of spiky scales under its chin that darkens when it feels threatened or excited. Bearded dragons are active during the day and spend time basking on rocks. They eat insects when young and more plants as adults.

Habitat:
Dry woodlands and desert scrub

Region:
Australia

Diet:
Omnivore (insects, leaves, flowers)

Size:
16–24 in (41–61 cm)

DID YOU KNOW?
Bearded dragons communicate by bobbing their heads and waving their arms. They can also puff up their bodies when startled.

Chuckwalla

Sauromalus ater

The chuckwalla is a large desert lizard known for its loose, baggy skin. When threatened, it wedges itself into rock crevices and inflates its body to stay tightly in place. Chuckwallas are active during the day and enjoy basking in the sun. They eat leaves, flowers, and fruits found in dry rocky habitats.

Habitat:
Rocky desert terrain

Region:
Southwestern North America

Diet:
Herbivore (leaves, fruits, flowers)

Size:
10–16 in (25–41 cm)

DID YOU KNOW?
When scared, a chuckwalla squeezes into a rock crevice and fills its lungs with air until it is wedged in too tight to be pulled out.

22

Collared Lizard

Crotaphytus collaris

The collared lizard is one of the most striking reptiles in North American deserts, with bright green and yellow scales and bold black bands around its neck. It can run on its two back legs at high speed, a rare ability among lizards. Males are highly territorial and bob their heads aggressively to warn off rivals. Collared lizards are active hunters that chase down insects and even other lizards.

Habitat:
Rocky deserts and scrubland

Region:
Southwestern United States, Mexico

Diet:
Carnivore (insects, small lizards)

Size:
8–14 in (20–36 cm)

DID YOU KNOW?
Collared lizards can stand upright and sprint on two legs. Males often display bright colors during the breeding season.

23

Desert Iguana

Dipsosaurus dorsalis

The desert iguana is one of the most heat-tolerant lizards in North America. It remains active even when temperatures rise above 100°F. With pale scales that reflect sunlight, it blends into desert sand and shrubs. Desert iguanas feed mainly on leaves and flowers, especially from creosote bushes.

Habitat:
Sandy and rocky desert

Region:
Southwestern United States, Mexico

Diet:
Herbivore (leaves, flowers, buds)

Size:
10–16 in (25–41 cm)

DID YOU KNOW?
The desert iguana can stay active at temperatures above 115 degrees Fahrenheit, higher than almost any other lizard in North America.

24

Desert Tortoise

Gopherus agassizii

The desert tortoise spends most of its life in underground burrows that protect it from extreme heat. It moves slowly but is well adapted to dry environments, storing water in its bladder for long periods. Desert tortoises eat grasses, flowers, and cactus pads. They are important animals that help shape desert plant communities.

Habitat:
Desert scrub and rocky slopes

Region:
Southwestern United States, Mexico

Diet:
Herbivore (grasses, flowers, cacti)

Size:
9–15 in (23–38 cm)

DID YOU KNOW?

When a desert tortoise feels threatened, it empties its bladder as a defense, releasing the stored water it depends on for survival.

25

Diamondback Rattlesnake

Crotalus atrox

The western diamondback rattlesnake is one of the largest and most recognizable venomous snakes in North America. Named for the distinctive diamond-shaped pattern along its back, it warns predators by shaking the hollow segments at the tip of its tail to produce its famous rattle. Diamondbacks are ambush hunters that detect prey using heat-sensing pits on their face, striking with precision at rodents, rabbits, and birds.

Habitat:
Desert scrub and rocky terrain

Region:
Southwestern United States, Mexico

Diet:
Carnivore (rodents, birds)

Size:
3.5–5 ft (1.1–1.5 m)

DID YOU KNOW?
A rattlesnake gains a new rattle segment each time it sheds its skin, which can happen several times in a single year.

Frilled Lizard

Chlamydosaurus kingii

The frilled lizard survives in the harshest dry scrublands and desert edges of Australia and New Guinea, where it relies on dramatic displays rather than speed for defense. When threatened, it reveals a wide frill of skin around its neck that fans out to make it look far more dangerous than it is. It also runs upright on its hind legs when escaping predators. When the bluff works, it simply folds its frill back and goes about its day.

Habitat:
Dry woodland and desert scrub

Region:
Australia and New Guinea

Diet:
Carnivore (insects, small lizards)

Size:
2–3 ft (60–90 cm)

DID YOU KNOW?
When a frilled lizard opens its mouth to hiss, its neck frill automatically fans outward at the same time, making the display and the threat happen together.

Gila Monster

Heloderma suspectum

The Gila monster is one of only a few venomous lizards in the world and the largest native lizard in the United States. It moves slowly and spends most of its life underground, but can deliver a powerful bite when threatened. Gila monsters store fat in their thick tails to survive long periods without food, sometimes going months between meals in the wild.

Habitat:
Desert scrub and rocky terrain

Region:
Southwestern United States, Mexico

Diet:
Carnivore (eggs, small mammals)

Size:
18–24 in (46–61 cm)

DID YOU KNOW?

A compound found in Gila monster saliva has been used to develop a real medication that helps people manage type 2 diabetes.

Horned Lizard

Phrynosoma platyrhinos

Horned lizards are squat, spiky reptiles that look more like tiny dinosaurs than typical lizards. They rely on camouflage as their first line of defense, blending almost perfectly into sandy desert soil. When that fails, they have a remarkable backup plan: they can squirt blood from their eyes to confuse and repel predators. Their diet consists almost entirely of ants.

Habitat:
Sandy desert and scrub

Region:
North America

Diet:
Carnivore (mostly ants)

Size:
3–5 in (8–13 cm)

DID YOU KNOW?
The horned lizard can squirt blood from its eyes up to five feet. The blood contains chemicals that taste foul to dogs, coyotes, and wolves.

29

Leopard Gecko

Eublepharis macularius

The leopard gecko is a small, spotted lizard that is active at night. It hides in cool burrows during the day to escape heat. Leopard geckos have eyelids, unlike many lizards, and use their sticky tongues to clean their eyes. They feed mainly on insects and rely on quiet, careful movements to catch prey.

Habitat:
Rocky deserts, dry grasslands

Region:
Middle East, South Asia

Diet:
Carnivore (insects, worms)

Size:
7–10 in (18–25 cm)

DID YOU KNOW?
If a leopard gecko loses its tail escaping a predator, it can grow a full replacement over the following months.

30

Monitor Lizard

Varanus griseus

The desert monitor is a large, fast-moving lizard with strong limbs and sharp claws. It explores wide territories in search of food and can run at impressive speeds when chasing prey. Desert monitors use their long, forked tongues to detect scents in the air. They are skilled hunters that climb, dig, and swim when needed.

Habitat:
Desert, savanna, rocky terrain

Region:
Africa, Asia, and Australia

Diet:
Carnivore (small mammals, birds)

Size:
2–7 ft (0.6–2.1 m)

DID YOU KNOW?
Monitor lizards have a forked tongue like a snake that they flick out to smell the air around them.

31

Sand Boa

Eryx colubrinus

The sand boa is a short, thick-bodied snake that spends most of its time hidden beneath loose sand. Its smooth scales help it glide underground where it waits to ambush passing prey. Sand boas are gentle, slow-moving snakes that rely on stealth rather than speed. They hunt small mammals and lizards in desert habitats.

Habitat:
Sandy deserts and dunes

Region:
North Africa, Middle East, Central Asia

Diet:
Carnivore (rodents, lizards)

Size:
18–30 in (46–76 cm)

DID YOU KNOW?
Sand boas are powerful burrowers that disappear quickly beneath sand. Their eyes sit high on their heads, allowing them to peek out while hidden.

Sidewinder Rattlesnake

Crotalus cerastes

The sidewinder is a small rattlesnake famous for its unusual way of moving across loose sand. Rather than slithering forward, it throws its body in a series of sideways loops that keep most of its surface off the hot ground at any one time. This keeps it cool and gives it excellent traction on shifting desert dunes. Small horns above its eyes help shade them from the desert sun.

Habitat: Sandy deserts and dunes

Region: Southwestern United States, Mexico

Diet: Carnivore (rodents, lizards)

Size: 18–30 in (46–76 cm)

DID YOU KNOW?

The sidewinder's unusual movement leaves a distinctive J-shaped track in the sand that makes it easy to identify exactly where it has traveled.

33

Thorny Devil

Moloch horridus

Despite its fearsome name, the thorny devil is a harmless lizard found in the dry deserts of Australia. Its entire body is covered in sharp spines that deter predators and serve another surprising purpose: channeling water. Tiny grooves between the spines direct moisture straight to the lizard's mouth, allowing it to drink through its skin after rain or morning dew. It eats almost nothing but small black ants.

Habitat:
Sandy desert scrub

Region:
Australia

Diet:
Carnivore (ants)

Size:
6–8 in (15–20 cm)

DID YOU KNOW?
Thorny devils can eat thousands of ants in a single day. Their "false head" on the back of their neck confuses predators.

BIRDS

Desert birds have mastered the challenge of surviving in a landscape with little shade, scarce water, and extreme heat. From ground-dwelling roadrunners to soaring eagles, they have developed behaviors and bodies that let them thrive where few other birds can.

34

Burrowing Owl

Athene cunicularia

The burrowing owl lives underground in old rodent burrows instead of tree nests. It stands tall on long legs and hunts insects and small animals in open desert landscapes. Unlike most owls, burrowing owls are active during the day. They remain alert near their burrow entrances and bob their heads when alarmed.

Habitat:
Desert grasslands and scrub

Region:
North and South America

Diet:
Carnivore (insects, small mammals)

Size:
7–10 in (18–25 cm)

DID YOU KNOW?

Burrowing owls often decorate their burrows with dung to attract insects. They also mimic rattlesnake sounds to scare predators.

35

Cactus Wren

Campylorhynchus brunneicapillus

The cactus wren is a loud, bold desert bird that builds large nests in thorny cactus plants. It is active during the day and feeds on insects, fruits, and seeds. Cactus wrens live in pairs or small families and fiercely defend their territory. Their scratchy, repetitive calls can be heard across desert landscapes.

Habitat:
Desert scrub and cactus habitat

Region:
Southwestern United States, Mexico

Diet:
Omnivore (insects, fruit, seeds)

Size:
7–8 in (18–20 cm)

DID YOU KNOW?
The cactus wren builds several decoy nests around its territory to confuse predators about which one it actually uses for sleeping and nesting.

36

Elf Owl

Micrathene whitneyi

The elf owl is the smallest owl in the world, standing no taller than a sparrow. It makes its home in the Sonoran Desert, often nesting inside holes in saguaro cacti that were carved out by woodpeckers. Elf owls hunt at night, catching insects, scorpions, and small lizards with impressive speed and precision. Despite their tiny size, they migrate thousands of miles each year between the U.S. and Mexico.

Habitat:
Desert scrub and saguaro cactus

Region:
Southwestern North America

Diet:
Carnivore (insects, scorpions)

Size:
4–5 in (10–13 cm)

DID YOU KNOW?
Rather than killing scorpions before eating them, the elf owl bites off the stinger first and swallows the rest of the scorpion alive.

Gambel's Quail

Callipepla gambelii

Gambel's quail are desert birds known for the single feather plume that curves forward on their heads. They travel in groups called coveys and forage for seeds and insects on the ground. These quail prefer running instead of flying and stay close to shrubs for protection. Their soft calls help keep the group together.

Habitat:
Desert scrublands, river washes

Region:
Southwestern United States, Mexico

Diet:
Omnivore (seeds, insects, berries)

Size:
10–12 in (25–30 cm)

DID YOU KNOW?
The feathery plume on a Gambel's quail's head is called a topknot and is made of just six overlapping feathers.

38

Golden Eagle

Aquila chrysaetos

The golden eagle is one of the most powerful birds of prey in the Northern Hemisphere. It soars over deserts and mountains with sharp eyesight that can spot prey far below. Golden eagles hunt rabbits, ground squirrels, and sometimes larger animals. They build large nests on cliffs and return to them year after year.

Habitat:
Open desert and mountain cliffs

Region:
North America, Europe, Asia

Diet:
Carnivore (mammals, birds, reptiles)

Size:
26–40 in (66–102 cm)

DID YOU KNOW?

A golden eagle can spot prey from nearly two miles away and has been recorded diving at speeds exceeding 150 miles per hour.

39

Greater Roadrunner

Geococcyx californianus

The greater roadrunner is a fast-running desert bird known for chasing lizards, snakes, and insects. It prefers staying on the ground rather than flying and uses its long legs to sprint across open areas. Roadrunners are active during the day and rely on speed and sharp vision to catch prey. They nest in shrubs and low trees.

Habitat:
Desert scrub and open country

Region:
Southwestern United States, Mexico

Diet:
Carnivore (insects, lizards, snakes)

Size:
20–24 in (51–61 cm)

DID YOU KNOW?
Roadrunners regularly hunt and kill rattlesnakes, pinning the snake's head and beating it against the ground before swallowing it whole.

40

Harris's Hawk

Parabuteo unicinctus

Harris's hawks are unique because they hunt cooperatively in small groups, unlike most raptors. Their teamwork helps them take down larger prey in open desert habitats. They perch on tall cacti or fence posts to scan for movement. These hawks use sharp talons and strong beaks to catch mammals, reptiles, and birds.

Habitat:
Desert scrub and semi-arid woodland

Region:
Southwest North America, South America

Diet:
Carnivore (small mammals, birds)

Size:
18–24 in (46–61 cm)

DID YOU KNOW?
Harris's hawks will sometimes stand on top of each other while perching, stacking two or three birds on the same post to get a better view of the surrounding desert.

41

Ostrich

Struthio camelus

The ostrich is the largest and heaviest bird in the world, built for running at high speeds across open deserts. Its long legs and strong muscles allow it to sprint away from predators. Ostriches cannot fly, but they defend themselves with powerful kicks. They feed on plants, seeds, and small animals.

Habitat:
Open desert and savanna

Region:
Africa

Diet:
Omnivore (plants, seeds, insects)

Size:
Up to 9 ft tall (2.7 m)

DID YOU KNOW?
Ostriches can run up to 45 miles per hour. An ostrich's eye measures nearly two inches across, making it the largest eye of any land animal on Earth.

Sandgrouse

Pterocles orientalis

Sandgrouse are desert birds that fly long distances to reach water sources. Their special belly feathers soak up water, which they carry back to their chicks. Sandgrouse feed mainly on seeds and travel in flocks for safety. Their fast, direct flight helps them avoid predators in open landscapes.

Habitat:
Sandy desert and dry grassland

Region:
Africa, Middle East, Central Asia

Diet:
Herbivore (seeds)

Size:
9–16 in (23–41 cm)

DID YOU KNOW?
Male sandgrouse fly up to 50 miles to reach watering holes, soak their specially adapted belly feathers, and return so their chicks can drink directly from the feathers.

Turkey Vulture

Cathartes aura

The turkey vulture is a large scavenging bird that soars high above desert landscapes searching for carrion. It uses an excellent sense of smell to locate food, something rare among birds. Turkey vultures rely on rising warm air currents to glide effortlessly with minimal wing flapping. They help keep ecosystems clean by removing dead animals.

Habitat:
Deserts, grasslands, open country

Region:
North and South America

Diet:
Carnivore (carrion)

Size:
25–32 in (64–81 cm)

DID YOU KNOW?
Turkey vultures cool themselves by spreading their wings in the sun. They rarely need to flap while flying, saving lots of energy.

INSECTS & ARTHROPODS

Scorpions, spiders, beetles, and centipedes may be small, but they are some of the toughest creatures in the desert. Their armored bodies resist moisture loss, and many can go months without food or water while enduring temperatures that would kill larger animals.

Bark Scorpion

Centruroides sculpturatus

The bark scorpion is the most venomous scorpion in North America, but it usually avoids humans and hides in cool, shaded places during the day. It hunts insects and small spiders at night, using its sensitive hairs to detect movement. Bark scorpions can climb walls and trees, making them skilled predators in desert habitats.

Habitat: Desert scrub and rocky terrain

Region: Southwestern United States, Mexico

Diet: Carnivore (insects, spiders)

Size: 2–3 in (5–8 cm)

DID YOU KNOW?
The bark scorpion is the only scorpion in the United States that regularly climbs vertical surfaces and is often found on walls and ceilings rather than the ground.

45

Camel Spider

Galeodes arab

Camel spiders are fast-moving desert hunters known for their large jaws and strong legs. Despite myths, they are not deadly to humans and are not true spiders. These predators hunt at night, chasing insects, small reptiles, and even other arachnids. They stay hidden during the day to avoid extreme heat.

Habitat:
Dry deserts and scrublands

Region:
Middle East and North Africa

Diet:
Carnivore (insects, lizards, rodents)

Size:
Up to 6 in (15 cm)

DID YOU KNOW?
Despite their fearsome appearance, camel spiders are not venomous. They are fast enough to chase down insects, small lizards, and even small birds.

46

Darkling Beetle

Eleodes armata

Darkling beetles are common desert insects known for their hard shells and slow, steady movements. They feed on dry plant material and help break down dead vegetation. Some species remain active during the day, while others avoid heat by emerging at night. Their sturdy bodies allow them to survive in harsh, sandy environments.

Habitat:
Sandy and rocky desert

Region:
Worldwide in arid regions

Diet:
Omnivore (decaying plant matter)

Size:
0.5–1.5 in (1–4 cm)

DID YOU KNOW?
Some darkling beetles raise their rear end to collect moisture from fog. They play an important role in recycling nutrients in desert ecosystems.

Desert Tarantula

Aphonopelma chalcodes

The desert tarantula is a large, hairy spider that spends much of its life in burrows underground. It hunts at night, using sensitive hairs to detect vibrations from prey. Tarantulas rarely bite unless threatened and rely on stealth rather than speed. They feed mainly on insects and other small animals.

Habitat:
Desert scrub and grassland

Diet:
Carnivore (insects, small lizards)

Region:
Southwestern United States, Mexico

Size:
3–4 in (8–10 cm)

DID YOU KNOW?

Female desert tarantulas can live up to 25 years, making them one of the longest-lived spiders in the world. Males rarely survive more than a year after reaching maturity.

Giant Desert Centipede

Scolopendra heros

The giant desert centipede is a large, fast-moving predator with many legs and strong venomous claws. It hunts insects, spiders, and even small vertebrates. Centipedes stay hidden during the day and emerge at night to search for prey. Their flexible bodies allow them to squeeze into tight spaces in desert rocks and soil.

Habitat:
Desert scrub and rocky areas

Region:
Southwestern United States, Mexico

Diet:
Carnivore (insects, lizards, rodents)

Size:
6–8 in (15–20 cm)

DID YOU KNOW?
The giant desert centipede injects venom through modified front claws and has been known to prey on animals much larger than itself, including small bats and lizards.

AMPHIBIANS

Amphibians seem like unlikely desert survivors — most need water to breathe and reproduce. Yet a handful of remarkable species have found ways to beat the odds, timing their entire lives around rare rainfall and disappearing underground for months at a time.

Desert Rain Frog

Breviceps macrops

The desert rain frog is a small, round amphibian known for its loud squeaking call. It lives along foggy coastal deserts where moisture collects on sand dunes. This frog spends most of its time buried just below the surface to stay cool and hydrated. It feeds on insects and emerges mainly at night.

Habitat:
Sandy coastal desert

Region:
Namibia, South Africa

Diet:
Carnivore (insects, larvae)

Size:
1.5–2 in (4–5 cm)

DID YOU KNOW?
The desert rain frog produces a surprisingly loud, high-pitched squeak as a defensive warning, which sounds quite unlike the call of any other frog.

50

Spadefoot Toad

Scaphiopus couchii

The spadefoot toad spends most of its life underground, emerging only after heavy desert rains. It breeds quickly in temporary pools that form during storms. Spadefoot toads use the hard, spade-shaped structures on their back feet to dig into soft soil. They feed on insects and stay hidden during dry periods to conserve moisture.

Habitat:
Desert scrub and grassland

Region:
Western United States, Mexico

Diet:
Carnivore (insects, worms)

Size:
1.5–3 in (4–8 cm)

DID YOU KNOW?
Spadefoot toads can transform from tadpoles to adults in just days during short desert rains. Their skin absorbs water directly from the soil.

DESERT ANIMAL RECORD BREAKERS

The desert is one of the most extreme environments on Earth, and the animals that live there are among the most extraordinary. From the fastest runner in the Western Hemisphere to a bird smaller than your fist, here are some of the most remarkable record holders in this book.

FASTEST

PRONGHORN

The pronghorn can sustain speeds of 55 miles per hour for several miles at a stretch, making it the fastest land animal in the Western Hemisphere.

TALLEST

OSTRICH

The ostrich stands up to nine feet tall and weighs up to 320 pounds, making it the largest and tallest bird on Earth. It cannot fly, but its powerful legs can carry it at speeds of 45 miles per hour and deliver a kick strong enough to kill a lion.

MOST VENOMOUS
BARK SCORPION

The bark scorpion is the most venomous scorpion in North America. Unlike most scorpions, it climbs vertical surfaces and is often found on walls and ceilings rather than the ground.

HEAVIEST
DROMEDARY CAMEL

The dromedary camel can weigh up to 1,320 pounds, making it the heaviest animal in this book. Despite its size, it can travel over 100 miles in a single day across open desert.

SMALLEST
DARKLING BEETLE

The darkling beetle measures as little as half an inch long, making it the smallest animal in this book.

BIGGEST EARS
FENNEC FOX

The fennec fox has enormous ears that can grow up to six inches long. These ears help release heat to keep the fox cool and allow it to hear small animals moving under the sand.

MOST LEGS
GIANT CENTIPEDE

The giant desert centipede has 40 legs and uses all of them to run down prey including lizards, small frogs, and even bats.

LONGEST LIVED
DESERT TORTOISE

The desert tortoise can live for over 80 years, making it one of the longest-lived reptiles on Earth. Some individuals in the wild are estimated to be older than 100 years.

Desert Animal Quiz

TRUE OR FALSE

1. A camel stores water in its hump.
2. The elf owl is the smallest owl in the world.
3. Kangaroo rats need to drink water every day to survive.
4. The pronghorn is the fastest land animal on Earth.
5. The horned lizard can squirt blood from its eyes.
6. Dingoes are native to North America.
7. The desert tortoise can live for over 80 years.

MATCH THE FACT TO THE ANIMAL

Draw a line from each fact to the correct animal. Each animal is used only once.

Fact	Word Bank
Can spend nearly a year underground	Fennec Fox
Smallest canid in North America	Sidewinder Rattlesnake
Leaves J-shaped tracks in sand	Spadefoot Toad
Has the largest ears relative to body size	Kit Fox
Can regrow a lost tail	Meerkat
Stands guard and barks to warn its group	Leopard Gecko

Desert Animal Quiz

MULTIPLE CHOICE

8. Which animal collects water through its own skin?

   a) Sand cat b) Thorny devil c) Jerboa d) Sidewinder

9. How many humps does a dromedary camel have?

   a) None b) Three c) Two d) One

10. Which of these animals hunts cooperatively in groups?

    a) Bobcat b) Coyote c) Harris's hawk d) Golden eagle

11. What does the frilled lizard use its neck frill for?

    a) Attracting mates b) Cooling down c) Scaring predators d) Catching insects

12. Which desert animal can run on its two back legs?

    a) Horned lizard b) Collared lizard c) Gila monster d) Desert iguana

13. Where does the elf owl make its nest?

    a) In rock crevices b) Underground burrows c) Saguaro cactus holes d) Thorny shrubs

14. Which animal is immune to scorpion venom?

    a) Sand cat b) Pallid bat c) Meerkat d) Kit fox

15. How does the spadefoot toad survive long droughts?

    a) Stores water in its hump b) Burrows underground c) Migrates to wetter regions d) Collects dew on its skin

Answers: 1. False 2. True 3. False 4. False (Western Hemisphere only) 5. True 6. False 7. True; Match: Spadefoot Toad, Kit Fox, Sidewinder, Fennec Fox, Leopard Gecko, Meerkat; Multiple Choice: 8. b 9. d 10. c 11. c 12. b 13. c 14. c 15. b

Glossary

Adaptation — A physical feature or behavior that helps an animal survive in its environment.

Arid — Extremely dry, with very little rainfall. Most deserts are arid environments.

Camouflage — Coloring or patterns that help an animal blend into its surroundings and avoid being seen.

Carnivore — An animal that eats only meat.

Cold-blooded — An animal whose body temperature changes with its surroundings. Reptiles and amphibians are cold-blooded.

Crepuscular — Active mainly at dawn and dusk rather than during the day or night.

Dormancy — A state of deep rest in which an animal slows its body down to survive harsh conditions.

Ecosystem — A community of living things interacting with each other and their environment.

Endangered — At serious risk of becoming extinct in the wild.

Estivation — A period of dormancy during hot or dry conditions, similar to hibernation in winter.

Herbivore — An animal that eats only plants.

Nocturnal — Active mainly at night rather than during the day.

Omnivore — An animal that eats both plants and meat.

Predator — An animal that hunts and eats other animals.

Prey — An animal that is hunted and eaten by other animals.

Reptile — A cold-blooded animal with scaly skin that lays eggs on land. Lizards, snakes, and tortoises are reptiles.

Scavenger — An animal that feeds on dead animals rather than hunting live prey.

Species — A group of animals that share the same characteristics and can reproduce with each other.

Taxonomy — The science of classifying living things into groups based on their characteristics.

Venom — A toxic substance produced by some animals and delivered through a bite or sting.

Index

adaptations, 6–7
addax, 11
amphibians, 62–64
Arabian oryx, 12
arthropods, 56–61
Bactrian camel, 13
bark scorpion, 57, 66
bat, 27
bearded dragon, 31
beetle, 59, 66
bighorn sheep, 14
birds, 45–55
bobcat, 15
burrowing owl, 46
cactus wren, 47
camels, 13, 20, 66
camel spider, 58
centipede, 61, 67
chuckwalla, 32
collared lizard, 33
coyote, 16
darkling beetle, 59, 66
desert cottontail, 17
desert hedgehog, 18
desert iguana, 34
desert rain frog, 63
deserts
about, 9
regions, 4–5
desert tarantula, 60
desert tortoise, 35, 67
diamondback rattlesnake, 36
dingo, 19
dromedary camel, 20, 66
eagle, 50
elf owl, 48
fennec fox, 21, 67
fox
fennec, 21, 67
kit, 25
frilled lizard, 37
frog, 63
Gambel's quail, 49
giant desert centipede, 61, 67
gila monster, 38
golden eagle, 50
greater roadrunner, 51
Harris's hawk, 52
hawk, 52
hedgehog, 18
horned lizard, 39
iguana, 34
insects, 56–61
javelina, 22
jerboa, 23
kangaroo rat, 24
kit fox, 25
leopard gecko, 40
lizards, 31–34, 37–41, 44
mammals, 10–29
meerkat, 26
monitor lizard, 41
ostrich, 53, 65
owls, 46, 48
pallid bat, 27
peccary, 22
pronghorn, 28, 65
rat, 24
rattlesnake, 36, 43
record breakers, 65–67
reptiles, 30–44
roadrunner, 51
sand boa, 42
sand cat, 29
sandgrouse, 54
scorpion, 57, 66
sidewinder rattlesnake, 43
snakes, 36, 42, 43
spadefoot toad, 64
spiders, 58, 60
tarantula, 60
thorny devil, 44
toad, 64
tortoise, 35, 67
turkey vulture, 55
vulture, 55

About the 50 Amazing Animals Series

The 50 Amazing Animals series takes young readers on a journey through the most fascinating animal kingdoms on Earth. Each book features 50 incredible species, brought to life through stunning photography and surprising facts that will keep kids reading from cover to cover.

Whether you are exploring scorching deserts, lush rainforests, or your own backyard, every title in the series is designed to spark curiosity and build a deeper appreciation for the natural world.

Perfect for young nature lovers, classrooms, and home libraries.

Also in the Series

50 Amazing Backyard Animals

50 Amazing Rainforest Animals

(More titles coming soon)

www.ingramcontent.com/pod-product-compliance
Ingram Content Group UK Ltd.
Pitfield, Milton Keynes, MK11 3LW, UK
UKHW060116010826
14089UKWH00003B/21